Resizing Your Life:

Time To Move On?

Tips for Seniors on Transitioning
from the Old place to the New

Emily Matthews, RN

First paperback edition September 2024

ISBN 979-8-218-51192-0

Independently Published

Table of contents

Acknowledgments

Naomi B. for all your help in formatting and design.

Resizing Your Life:
Time To Move On?

Tips for Seniors on Transitioning from the Old place to the New

Emily Matthews, RN

CHAPTER ONE
Is it Time to Resize?

Is It Time?

Laura Ingalls once wrote, "Home is the nicest word there is." Anybody who's read her books knows how fondly she regarded the "home place." We all feel the same to a greater or lesser degree.

But…life happens, and sometimes staying in the current situation might not be working the way it should. That's when people may start to consider making a transition from one place to the next. Or when their family starts "bugging" them to move.

Chapter One – Time To Resize?

"I can't give up my home." It's easy to feel this way. "Home" represents memories, routine, safety. Even if it may not actually *be* safe, people tend to *feel* that way. Some procrastinate and stay in their homes too long for their own safety. Why?

First of all, even though an unsafe living situation appears obvious to family or to professionals, to the person living where they've always lived the place seems safe. Because it's *familiar.* Even when people may not be living the life they worked for or want, they tend to cling to the well-known.

There is also the illusion of control. A person may find their life limited by mobility issues, general health, even clutter or unsafe conditions, yet may put off seriously thinking about a move under the illusion that they have total control. Yet the exact opposite often happens when procrastination is taken to an extreme.

Karl was an example of a danger that could happen but didn't. A life-long bachelor, he managed pretty well at home even as he reached his 90s. Then he started falling. Each time, he was able to drag himself up by using furniture or a lawnmower or snowblower if it happened in the garage. His nephew would check on him frequently and each time he asked about the new bruise, Karl would minimize it.

Eventually his nephew, who worked in healthcare, had a talk with him. "Why don't you get a medical alert? What if you fell and couldn't get up?" Karl made all sorts of excuses, one being, "Well, the neighbors would notice and come help me."

But Karl didn't realize that "the neighbors" weren't all that interested in his activities. His nephew had to point that out, and finally convinced him to get the medical alert. Karl was able to stay at home safely because he wore it all the time once it arrived.

In contrast to this illustration, every fall and winter, we'd get ER patients that were found at home on the floor after lying there for days. They had put off moving because they didn't want to leave the familiar. They felt safe, but really weren't.

When they arrived, they'd be unconscious, injured, and hypothermic. Often it would be a mailman, not a neighbor, who noticed the mail piling up in the box, who called authorities. Sometimes it might be an out of town relative in the habit of calling weekly who noticed the patient hadn't answered. Of course, after being treated in ER, they'd be admitted to the hospital.

Upon discharge they were usually given nursing home placement at whatever facility could take them. Maybe some of them were only there for rehab. but I'm sure some of them never ended up "back home" again, especially if their injuries meant they couldn't get about anymore. They had put off making a move until the decision was no longer theirs.

If you find you just can't bring yourself to make a move yet, I'll be forceful here and say that if you have health issues such as falls and near misses, you must get a medical alert! It will buy you time to consider all your options.

The people who had those alerts didn't end up coming into ER, unless they were also injured when they fell. We'd hear calls on the scanner for "fell and can't get up" but the ambulance didn't have to bring them in. Having a medical alert meant these people were able to stay at home at least long enough to begin planning their own move in their own timing.

Options: You Might Not *Have* to Move Yet

Maybe you've considered making a move because the yardwork is becoming too heavy. Or you can no longer do stairs. If the home is in good repair, opting to stay a little longer might work.

For example, sometimes people tell me they want to move to a condo because they don't want maintenance. I usually ask, "If there was a way to stay where you are, would you prefer that, or do you really want to move?" If they tell me they're not sure, I may suggest that they pay someone to do the yardwork and shoveling, because that could end up being no more expensive than condo fees.

If there is enough money on hand, you might consider retrofitting the house with ramps, turning a dining room into a ground floor bedroom, or installing hookups for washer and dryer in a bedroom. This only makes sense if the house is not already starting to deteriorate. If there is any *deferred maintenance* (i.e. repairs that should have happened but didn't), selling the place before it deteriorates further is the best plan.

And doing so allows you to choose early on where you will be living. Even if you are OK in the current situation, you should look into other options before life takes a turn that limits your choices. Because procrastination is truly an enemy!

Procrastination: The Thief of Time

Why do people procrastinate when it comes to making a move in their senior years? Or even thinking about it? Usually, it's fear of the unknown in some way. Here are some examples:

- **Downsizing.** Some people have spent years accumulating and saving things that "might be useful." They can't bring themselves to let go of these things, especially for fear someone might want it.

- **Finances.** Fears about running out of money if a move is made, and the belief that staying in the home is "free."

- **The wrong decision.** Fear of making a mistake is a huge barrier to making any decision about anything.

Let's explore these fears and analyze what they mean. None of these need prevent making a move.

- Downsizing Can Seem Impossible! It's best to start doing it way before actually making a move. If you believe you'll be selling your home in the next year or two, please start clearing out *now.* You'll make it so much easier on yourself!

Collections:

Many people have collections or items they consider valuable. They save them "for the family" or just because they enjoy them. But to avoid potential future arguments and to make downsizing easier, enlist the help of your family.

Your first step will be to ask them outright if any of them want your special things. One way to deal with this is to have them make lists of items they want. Say there are four children, and you have 16 items they may want. If more than one wants an item, you could have a drawing, and then eliminate that name from the drawing for the next contested item.

Another way might be to sell the item if it's valuable and split the money. You may decide to leave different items to different people in your will.

Your family may surprise you with not wanting the items at all, but are afraid to tell you, in the belief it will hurt your feelings. You must be willing to accept that they may not want the things you believed they'd want.

You might also be shocked to find there's something they value, that you see little worth in! Whatever action you take, it's best to get input now while everyone can talk together about it. One resource that can be useful is **www.fairsplit.com**

Harry had an enormous collection. There were display cabinets in every room of the house, including the kitchen. Plus more in the basement. He had started packing some things and there were boxes in a spare bedroom before he even called me.

I knew prospective buyers would be intimidated by the collection, so I suggested he continue packing things up and move all boxes and display cabinets into the spare bedroom. That way, all the other rooms would have freed-up space and look more open for showings. And Harry was able to deal with the collection later after he moved, after finding a buyer for the items.

Sometimes a collection is so huge that an estate sale is needed. Ruby glass, flow blue, solid silver, beer signs,

Chapter One – Time To Resize?

Depression glass, model trains, jewelry, furniture…these may be more (or less) valuable than you think.

A good estate sale company will appraise and price, clean, organize, and display the items, and you will probably net more than if you tried to sell them on your own. Plus, they take care of clean-up afterward.

Estate sale companies get booked up fast, so call them early if a move is on the horizon. Often they are booked six months out in their timelines!

Most of the time, these companies want free rein in the home. They prefer doing the sale in vacant homes, so you'll have to plan ahead. If you haven't already moved into your new place, you may be asked to move out temporarily. That might be a good time to take a vacation if you're planning to stay after the sale.

There are also companies that sell everything online. They may not be able to sell the wide variety that happens with in-house sales, but they are an option for those who just need an easier process.

Rita had spent years collecting several types of antiques. She'd already started renting an apartment and was going back to the old place to do maintenance. Her house was crammed.

Initially she had considered placing sale ads, calling antique dealers, or even a rummage sale, but the dealers couldn't take the sheer volume. Her kids told her not to expect them to do a rummage sale, and were worried she might "give away" something for $15 that was worth much more.

They called a couple of estate sale companies, and picked one. Rita ended netting much more than she'd ever dreamed, which allowed her to use the money for other things she wanted to do. And her old home was now almost empty so she could list it without it looking cluttered. The furniture that was left to help stage the home, she donated after getting an offer.

Chapter One – Time To Resize?

"Stuff":

This would be everything else that you have–or that your kids parked in your house-that you don't consider especially valuable but have simply kept. I once sold a home where there were a dozen end tables! They weren't all in use; the owner just stored them in the basement, along with large numbers of kids' toys, carpet rolls, paint, tools, desks, and chairs. Dealing with this type of situation on top of moving causes stress.

Use your "pre-move" time to avoid that stress by downsizing and de-cluttering *now*. Tell the kids you are no longer "Dad's Warehouse" and that if they still want what they asked you to keep, to come get it by (date). And stick to the date!

If it's your own belongings that you really haven't used in some time, ask your family to take what they want. Offer things to neighbors. Your family can then collaborate with you to deal with the other things not claimed. You can categorize these into "keep," "donate," and "toss." Then keep, donate, and toss!

Bob asked me to help him sell his house. He'd managed to keep the house pretty tidy, except for a junk room. But his garage was a nightmare! Thigh-deep in clutter, tools, machines, and junk, it was a certain challenge. He really didn't know where to start and was somewhat disabled, so I asked him early on if he wanted clean-out people to help, and he agreed.

The problem was, Bob would come in during the sorting and grab an old newspaper or magazine, start looking at it, and then would decide it belonged in the *maybe* category. He'd do the same thing with broken tools and furniture, old windows, or old doorknobs with parts missing. That *maybe* pile got big in a hurry!

The day before closing, he was panicking. The *maybe* pile was still there! He'd procrastinated sorting it by himself as he'd promised he would. Plus, he hadn't cleaned out the junk room yet. The clean-out guys came to the rescue again, and all of Bob's *maybes* were tossed. There was no more time left.

NOTE: Be careful about using a *maybe* category, lest everything ends up there, resulting in not getting rid of anything.

- Finances Can Be Scary?

The illusion that "staying is free," especially if the home starts to deteriorate, is just that: an illusion. First, there will always be taxes and utilities to pay. Then the maintenance costs, such as roof replacement, painting or replacing windows, furnace or water heater replacement, or basement repairs are very real. If you own the equity in your home and appreciation has slowed down, your asset isn't working as well as it could if invested elsewhere.

Some people sell their home and invest the proceeds in an account, planning to use that to pay their monthly charge in their new place. Some worry they will run out of money when they need it most: for example, when the level of needed care rises. However, there are many facilities that do take Medicaid or waivers, so nobody is ever "left out on the street."

Chapter One – Time To Resize?

Regarding finances, it's a good idea to examine what your home is costing both monetarily and socially. It might help to ask yourself these questions:

- Have I put off paying for something I know needs to be done (e.g. new roof)?
- Am I embarrassed to have friends over due to the state of the house?
- Is it hard or impossible for me to do all the normal maintenance associated with homeownership?
- Is it difficult to find anybody that will do simple (or major) repairs?
- Are there health or mobility restrictions or any changes that are interfering with my use of the home (e.g. can't manage stairs anymore)?
- Is the home far from family, doctors, or shopping?
- Do I have old leaky windows or old siding?
- Are utilities hard to pay?

It could be best to get the money out of your home before it deteriorates further, and before health issues make it impossible to stay.

- The Wrong Decision?

Strangely, this fear is identical to the fear many first time buyers face. I tell everyone, "We all have fear, and we *will* all have some level of buyer's (or seller's) remorse. I know from experience. The important thing is to take that fear and own it, rather than letting the fear take you." In other words, it's important to avoid Analysis Paralysis.

Nobody can predict the future or know for certain that they'll be 100% happy in a new place, but you can definitely take steps to minimize unpleasant surprises. Develop an action plan based on what you know now. (And ask yourself, "When I moved into my current home, did I really *know* I'd be happy? Didn't *some* bad things happen here, too?")

Start by learning as much as you can about different living options. The more data you can gather, the better. Then, consider your current health and physical needs: will you maybe need more help as time goes on? Look for facilities that can *grow their care* as time progresses.

> Make new lists of pros and cons regarding moving each week and save them all in a designated place. Don't read the previous lists! After a month or two, take them all out and review them. You should notice certain themes or issues that come up again and again. You'll want to pay attention to those. This can help solidify your thinking about re-sizing.

The Fear You Actually Should Be Concerned About?

This is the fear of *losing control due to procrastination.* When people procrastinate long enough, they will end up in a situation where their choices are limited or non-existent. Procrastination can *feel* as if you are maintaining control by "not thinking about it." But really all it does is limit your options if taken too far.

When people are considering making a move, it takes a conscious decision on the part of all concerned. You may already have your own lists, but here are some I've come up with. General reasons to sell sooner rather than later include:

- You will have more options because of not waiting so long you're *forced* to move

- Sellers' market

- House too big or too small: size won't change by waiting

- Health concerns

- Economic/money concerns: is there still a mortgage? Are repairs left undone due to inability to pay?

- Upkeep concerns: avoiding future *certain* repairs. E.g. a roof that is "older but still functional" will be even older & need replacement by waiting. Then the property will be hard (or impossible) to sell unless a new roof is installed

- Lifestyle needs: the home is taking too much of your time to maintain, clean, etc.

- Need/want to be closer to family, doctors, shopping

- Inability to retrofit to accommodate changing mobility, e.g. stairs or inaccessible bathroom

General reasons to wait a little and think things over:

- Repairs that need to be made *now*: It's best to fix things first before listing

- Strong buyer's market

- Emotions: too soon in the *stages of decision making* (next chapter) to let go yet

- Not-so-good time of year: there are seasons that favor sellers

Some folks may never feel ready to move. Therefore, it's wise to start asking positive *what-ifs* like "What if I can see family more often?" or "What if I didn't have to shovel anymore in the winter?"

Ask yourself: would moving make life easier, help you regain time for hobbies, free you of home maintenance tasks? Is the life you currently live what you worked for all your life? Or are you more and more simply confined to your house?

Reflect on this and be ruthlessly honest with yourself regarding your projected future needs. Because you don't want to end up *having* to move and *not having* a choice.

Chapter One – Time To Resize?

CHAPTER TWO
Stages of Decision-Making

What if your spouse wants to move and you don't? What if *you* want to move and your spouse doesn't? What if you would prefer to stay put but your family is worried about the situation?

Here's something borrowed from healthcare: the concept of "stages." When someone gets an unwelcome diagnosis, they are observed to move through *stages of feeling or being,* until acceptance is reached. Just so, the *decision to move* goes through these stages also. These stages considered in the context of making a move are:

Denial: "I'm doing just fine here!" "My/his/her mobility isn't *that* bad yet." "My/our finances aren't *that* shaky; the bank wouldn't *really* foreclose!"

Anger: "Why does s/he/they want me to move!? How dare they!" "Why did life treat me/us so badly? I/We don't want to give this up!" "Interfering relatives!"

Bargaining: "I/We can probably put off those repairs for a while yet." "We'll just turn down the thermostat if it starts costing too much." "Can't you (i.e.family) just come over and help some more?" "I have plenty of time; I don't really have to move *that* soon."

Depression: This can take many forms, but really seems to be very fleeting in the case of planning a needed move. Some people skip right over this stage.

Acceptance: This is the stage when people start actively looking at alternative living arrangements. This is the fun stage! There really are a lot of opportunities for any budget.

In going through these stages it helps, as stated before, to ask rhetorical questions like "What if, instead of staying in a drafty, too-big place with high taxes and stairs, it could be traded for more freedom?" "What if the move meant being closer to the children or friends?" "What if moving meant not having to worry about all these bills?" Consider the following examples and see how each situation illustrates the *stages of decision making.*

Dale and Donna

They were the ultimate go-go-go couple. They'd built their house in the 60s and stayed there ever since. Though Dale had worked all his life as a mechanic, they managed their finances extremely well and had a sizeable nest egg: enough to afford multiple vacation trips after he retired. Donna had worked various part-time jobs and was a well-known volunteer for just about anything. In fact, they had to arrange all their trips around her volunteering!

But as time went on, they did slow down, until in their mid-80s, their activities were mostly trips to the mall or to see their extended family. Donna didn't go places on her own anymore and spent a lot of time just sleeping when they were at home together. She was also becoming more unsteady on her feet.

They continued living in their large home, and Dale was getting frustrated. He still had all the yardwork, home maintenance, car maintenance, bills, plus was now shouldering things Donna was unable or unwilling to do, like cooking at times or cleaning. There were many evenings Donna would just put off cooking supper until 9:30 PM.

Their extended family tried to help as much as possible, e.g. tree-trimming, repairs, raking, etc. But they had to travel over an hour to do so, and Dale "didn't want to bother them too much." Meanwhile, Donna was still going downstairs to the basement to do the laundry. Dale worried every time she did, but this was one chore she didn't want to let him do.

Finally, Dale had had enough. He told Donna they needed to move, but Donna became dramatic, saying things like, "You just don't know how much I love this house! How dare you tell me that?" and "I will never leave this place!" Dale backed down for a while, then finally, suddenly, Donna agreed to move to a senior community.

Once settled in their new community, they loved it! Donna never once expressed wanting to go back home and Dale was free to enjoy just living in a place where he didn't have to worry about storm windows, grass, taxes, roof, cleaning, shoveling, or Donna falling down basement stairs. They no longer needed a car because there were enough people in the area to take them places, and there was also the option of a senior taxi van (care van) in case nobody else could do it.

One great part of it was the meal plan. Since Donna no longer wanted to cook, they could walk to the hub of the campus and eat dinner there. They were free to use the exercise equipment and go for walks on the pedestrian trails. Everything was wheelchair-friendly so as Donna began to give up walking, they could still go places in the community. They maintained independence without the stress.

The best part was that now some of their extended family was less than a 20-minute drive away, instead of over an hour. As a result, they got a lot more visits from their kids, grandkids, and great-grandkids. Even the relatives that lived "up north" were able to drop by at times, because their trip time was cut in half.

"This place is great! We wish we'd moved sooner!" was their standard response to anybody who asked.

Kenny

Kenny lived alone since his wife died. He existed in a house full of memories and stuff. He called me as he felt taking care of his house was getting to be a burden.

When I arrived, I was stunned to find that in such a limited space, he'd managed to cram in eleven couches, large chairs, and loveseats, plus end tables, a dining table and chairs, and a card table. He kept making statements like "This place is getting too much for me. I'm thinking of downsizing. Stairs are getting hard."

We spoke briefly and one thing I suggested was having someone help him sort through and get rid of some of the "stuff." He answered, "Yes, of course, I know I have to move it all out once I sell the house."

Since I believed the house would be almost impossible to show without some of it gone ahead of time,

I suggested he start eliminating some of it "...now, because after all, in a smaller place it won't all fit anyway." His shocked look told me he hadn't thought of that, and that the truth about too much stuff was only now sinking in.

A few days later he called me to say he was 'just too stressed to think about moving." He hadn't been able to wrap his mind around getting rid of even *some* of the stuff.

Al

When we met, he confessed that he *had to* move. He'd bought the place later in life from his brother's estate and his house was immense for a single person to be living in. But the reason for selling wasn't re-sizing, as I imagined. Al had money troubles.

Assuming he owned it outright, the first thing I did was ask if he had heard about reverse mortgages, which nowadays are not the bad old product they were in the 1990s. My thought was that it would enable him to stay in his home and use the money to catch up on bills or pay for needed repairs.

He admitted that he didn't have enough equity for that to be a plan. In fact, if he tried to stay, he'd end up getting foreclosed on. His situation was dire.

Al was angry at life and had, in spite, started paying all bills with new credit cards that he'd taken out. Now the debt load was even bigger.

This complicated his search for a new place because he absolutely refused to consider low-income housing which he could have qualified for. Fortunately, Al's credit was still good enough that he could qualify for one type of loan, so we started looking for smaller houses.

But Al hadn't told the loan officer about a money judgement! Eventually when the truth came out, his buying power was further reduced because he had to pay it, and he was madder than ever.

He admitted that what he wanted was above his price point, but even then, he kept finding fault with every property that he could afford. He kept comparing everything to his current "mansion."

Because this occurred before the super-hot sellers market, he was able eventually to find something that he could afford that wasn't "awful." But…"It's terrible I have to move here!" He could find barely one thing that he saw as a positive about the new place.

Once moving day arrived, Al grudgingly took possession of his new home. I felt bad for him, but there was no other solution given his circumstances and choices.

About seven months later, he called, telling me how much he loved his new place. I was shocked because the issues necessitating his move had been anything but pleasant for him. Al reported the view was great, the back yard was big enough, he was getting to know the neighbors, and he didn't have to worry about stairs anymore! He was finally able to see the benefits of moving when he had, rather than waiting for foreclosure.

Frida

Frida and her husband had downsized from their huge home into a much smaller ranch. They enjoyed taking walks in their new surroundings and meeting with the neighbors. Unfortunately, shortly after the move her husband died.

Frida coped well enough, but began to exhibit classic signs of depression: tiredness, loss of interest in hobbies, and loss of appetite. Her sons were concerned that she wasn't eating much, but she claimed she needed to lose weight anyway. Then she became physically weak.

Frida started falling…frequently. Every time her medical device activated, whether day or night, one of her sons would get a call and go over to help her. This was getting old fast for all of them.

As she was a retired science teacher, Frida looked at her situation methodically and analytically. She decided that the best option would be for her to choose some sort of assisted living situation. Her sons wholeheartedly agreed.

Because she did have some time on her side, she was able to research and interview different options and got on the waiting list for her favorite pick. Frida was in complete control of her situation because her circumstances weren't immediately pressing.

And once she moved in, she started up her hobbies and socializing again. Her only regret was that they "hadn't moved into assisted living straight away instead of getting that smaller place. Moving twice stinks!"

The Decision to Re-size: The Acceptance Stage, aka the Fun Stage

Once you've decided to make a move, you will want to consider all your options. If you are pressed for time, this *could* limit your choices but it doesn't have to. I once sold a house for a 100-year-old who needed to move within two months, and she still was able to find what she wanted for her new accommodation.

When you are deciding to re-size, you will need to make practical choices. As in the example of Frida, going from a large 2-story to a small ranch may not end up being the most sensible decision if you or a partner already have diagnosed health issues. Doing that may mean having to move twice.

On the other hand, if there is good reason to believe that the stay in the new place will be for quite some time, then buying a ranch, "twindominium" or condo can be an excellent plan. Just make sure to explore all the resources available in your county that can allow you to stay there as long as you want. The next chapter discusses the many other living options available.

CHAPTER THREE
Where to Go?

The type of new place you choose will be a function of finances, functionality, location, and future expectations. For example, if you or your spouse has a medical condition that will require increasing levels of care, you'll want to make sure the place you select has options for that. Your County's Aging and Disability Resource Center (ADRC) should have information on all the different types of housing.

Many people who decide to re-size are considering some form of senior community instead of yet another house. After all, their goal is to simplify their life and cut down on maintenance! The different types of housing are:

- Income based. Open to anybody who meets the Income requirements

- Senior condos

- Senior apartments, income-based or not income-based

- Assisted living

We'll explore each type below.

Income-based

If you are facing a low-income situation, besides opportunities for senior housing, there is section 8. One couple that was finding remaining in their home too difficult financially were able to sell and rent from a Section 8 landlord. If the idea of a larger complex doesn't appeal to you, you can see about getting on a Section 8 housing list as they did. While fairly rare, there may be a landlord that will rent to you.

Senior Condos

There are some places that have condos to rent, not buy. These condos are for those who want truly independent living. Some facilities may allow the condo tenants to eat at the main campus if they also incorporate an RCAC at that site. If medical needs change, a person can move from the condo into the apartment for greater levels of care and remain on the same campus.

Senior Apartments, either Income- or not Income-based

There are different types of these. Some are high-rise and some are "cottage- style;" almost like a ground level string of condos. These are for seniors who are independent, and they don't offer meals.

However, some of them may organize field trips, and often the residents themselves plan get-togethers: groups for sewing, card playing, or potlucks, for example.

Assisted Living

Assisted living refers to three types of facilities: Residential Care Apartment Complex (RCAC), Community Based Residential Facility (CBRF), and Adult Family Home (AFH). WI statutes relating to them can be found below.

- docs.legis.wisconsin.gov/code/admin_code/dhs/030/89
- www.dhs.wisconsin.gov/regulations/assisted-living/survey.htm
- docs.legis.wisconsin.gov/code/admin_code/dhs/030/83/_1
- docs.legis.wisconsin.gov/code/admin_code/dhs/030/88
- DQA map: www.dhs.wisconsin.gov/dqa/bal-regionalmap.htm

RCAC

RCACs serve those who want to maintain independence but also have the security of onsite staff, and the option to have meals onsite. They can be Certified or Registered. Certified RCACs can take both private pay and Medicaid-eligible residents ("...shall comply with all other applicable requirements of the Medicaid Community Waivers Manual" WI DHS 89.52)

Registered RCACs may be inspected at any time by DHS, but they are not *routinely* inspected. They are not required to have a contract with the county agency that administers the medical assistance waiver.

All RCACs are required to have full kitchens, private bathrooms, living, and sleeping areas in the apartments. They must have their own private entrance and exit, and are to be physically separated from any CBRF or nursing home that may also be on the campus.

There will be a comprehensive assessment prior to being admitted, which will include physical, nutritional, mental/emotional, behavioral/social, and monitoring needs. The RCAC will then develop a service agreement in collaboration with the tenant, which must include details about services, fees, and policies and procedures. The service agreement may be updated at the request of the tenant or facility, or when there is a change in the comprehensive assessment.

For a list of RCACs, you may refer to the information provided by your County's ADRC or go to **www.dhs.wisconsin.gov/guide/rcacdir.pdf**

CBRF

CBRFs have a higher level of care than RCACs. For example, RCACs are not allowed to have tenants with an activated POA for Healthcare, but CBRFs are allowed. RCACs cannot have residents with court-appointed guardians, but CBRFs can.

CBRFs require an initial assessment similar to that for RCACs, and there are different classes of CRBFs: A, AS, ANA, CA, CS, and CNA. They are licensed according to size: small, medium, and large. Who may stay in them is governed by what class they are.

A CRBF is a more cozy arrangement than a RCAC because they have a higher level of care.

Normally a resident in a CBRF has a room with an en suite bathroom, but no kitchen as in RCACs. Meals are taken in the dining room, and there are common areas like large living rooms, where people can congregate. There are no options for residents to cook in a CBRF, but most folks do have a small apartment size refrigerator.

Residents can be responsible for taking any medication they have, but in reality, most residents in CBRFs are given their medications, instead of self-taking them. CBRFs are required to monitor residents' health and maintain medical records.

For a list of CBRFs, you may refer to information provided by your County's ADRC or go to **www.dhs.wisconsin.gov/guide/cbrfdir.pdf**

AFH

AFHs are also known as *group homes* and are listed according to the population they serve. Many of them are not specifically for seniors, but there are some that cater to "advanced age." According to DHS 88, an AFH is "...a place where 3 or 4 adults not related to the licensee reside..." Some of them take public funding.

Many other requirements are similar to RCACs and CBRFs. AFHs can allow pets. For a list of AFHs, you may refer to information provided by your County's ADRC or go to **www.dhs.wisconsin.gov/guide/afhdir.pdf**

Questions to ask and info to know about assisted living:

Fees:

- Does the facility accept public funding?
- Deposit/application fee/entrance fee?
- Rent, meals, services: what are each of these?
- Monthly rate for services?
- Are there *levels* of services and how does the cost increase if the person's level increases?
- Any extra services? Charges?
- What is the refund policy?

Scheduling:

- What times are meals served?

- What time does the podiatrist/OT/PT come (if they have these)?

- If there's a care van, are there times when it doesn't run?

- What is the activity calendar like? (Get them to show you)

- If there are church services or other structured gatherings, where and when are they?

- If there are organized field trips, when are they and how many per year?

Space:

- Room dimensions?

- If there are different prices, are there different sizes?

- How far is it to walk to dining/shopping/beauty parlor/etc?

- How big are the common areas? Where are they?

- What kind of parking is available?

Food:

- Ask for a *list* of all meals served in the past week, not just a "sample menu"
- How equipped are they for special diets such as GF, DF, egg-free, no dyes, kosher, halal, etc?
- Can families supply special foods for the resident if needed?

Staffing:

- What are the nurse's hours?
- Does the facility have any other on-site healthcare staff besides the caregivers?
- Who are they and what are their hours?
- Are all staff gait-belt trained? (if applicable)

Amenities:

- Are pets ever allowed?
- Is WIFI or cable included or contracted separately?
- Pool?
- Exercise room?
- Shops/snack places?
- Beauty parlor?

- Walking trail?
- Outside patios?

Care/Service plans:

- Ensure you and your family read over the care plan and make sure everything is addressed that needs to be
- Ask for updates periodically
- If mobility changes, check to see the plan is updated to reflect safety measures such as chair alarms, or wheelchairs to get to the dining area
- Take nothing for granted! If the staff don't appear to be open when you are first talking to them or when settling in, you may need to probe for answers.

Roger was an ER nurse. His sister was an optometrist and his brother a dentist. When it came time for their mother to go into assisted living due to dementia, Roger asked if the staff would monitor his mom's blood sugar as she was on oral hypoglycemics.

His siblings quickly shut down that query as they felt they outranked him degree-wise, and "...she's not checking it now, is she? What's the point?"

Roger acquiesced but asked the staff to make sure they would check her blood sugar if it ever seemed warranted (PRN). The staff assured him they would, and that they would add this to the care plan. Except they didn't.

One day Roger was notified that his mother was unresponsive and probably dying.

Because he lived the closest, he started on his way to the facility. As he drove, he started wondering what her blood sugar was, because that is the first, most logical reason for any diabetic to be unresponsive.

Upon arrival, he asked what the blood sugar was, and was met with a blank stare. "She doesn't have a glucometer assigned to her." Shocked, he asked if they had one for emergencies; they didn't. "And we can't do that because it's not on her care plan." Roger stepped outside and called 911.

As he'd suspected, his mom's blood sugar was dangerously low, but quickly reversed by the paramedics. She had to stay in the hospital until she was stable (5 days). Roger felt vindicated that he'd asked the right questions at the beginning, and this time his siblings agreed. They all examined the new care plan to ensure it contained the correct information.

Chapter Three – Where To Go?

CHAPTER FOUR
Family Matters

Family Input

Suppose you've decided to re-size. You have ideas about where your new place will be and have started information-gathering. You call your kids to come help with downsizing the stuff and...they are *shocked*. Instead of congratulating you on your foresight, they express angst. "You *can't* sell that house! We grew up there!" or "You're only 67: why do you want to move *now*?" or "What's wrong with where you're living now?"

Believe it or not, this can happen. Because they don't want to give up their memories or feelings of comfort derived from meeting at Mom's place for the holidays. Maybe one was hoping to be able to buy the house, but can't swing it financially. Whatever the reasons, your family also has to work through the *stages of decision making,* and come to terms with life changes. Remember that though they may have feelings about the place, it really is your decision.

On the other hand, many seniors have decided to re-size only after many suggestions were made by family members. In this case, the family may express such enthusiasm about the news that the senior feels pressured. It's important to remind your family in this scenario that you need time to go through the process, especially if there's a lot of sorting to do. You can tell them they'll have to help if they want it to happen faster than your projected timeline.

At times, the decision to re-size is complicated by a "committee" with siblings, children, nieces, nephews, grandkids all wanting to chime in. This is understandably intricate. When so many people want to have a say in what happens, it can become difficult to make any decisions at all.

I have been in these situations, and what seems to work best is to have a round table discussion (literally everyone sitting in a circle), where everyone is asked to express themselves. Take notes; it helps.

After that, the homeowner can thank everyone for their input, and go on to make a decision. Even if the decision isn't what some of the committee want, they can be assured that their concerns were heard. You don't have to answer to all the relatives when it's *your* home.

Family vs Professionals: Packing & Prep Work

Sometimes seniors who are used to *doing it all on their own* hesitate to ask family for help with packing. Either they "don't want to bother" anybody or they see doing it all on their own almost as a badge of honor.

When touch-ups or actual repairs are needed, the situation could get even stickier. Be honest with yourself: is it *really* safe to go up that ladder? If you have a bad back, *should* you be lifting those things? It won't help at all if you end up in the hospital with injuries because you felt the need to do it all alone. (And if you are on any blood thinners, the situation could end up even worse than feeling sore the next day).

My intention is not to be alarmist but I really have had patients that fell off ladders resulting in brain hemorrhage. Or had something heavy fall on them when they tried to move it, resulting in a crushed joint necessitating joint replacement.

Bud had spent his whole life working for his family. He did all the home repairs, car maintenance, and yardwork. When a family member had to make an international move, he organized it all.

When he replaced the roof, he'd arranged with the roofer to pull off the old roof on his home "to save money" so all the roofer had to do was install the new one. He could fix or build almost anything, and built a shed in his late 70s.

But an old injury meant that he had a bad back. It didn't affect him much, so he just kept going. When it was time to re-size in his 90s, he had many helpers who made sure he didn't try to lift anything, because by now, his back did bother him.

Unfortunately, Bud decided "just to move something light" when they were all busy elsewhere. He suffered compression fractures in his back, and had to be on pain killers the rest of his life.

The best way to get things packed whether simply downsizing/decluttering or packing for a move is to get others involved, whether family members or professionals. There are pros and cons to each method.

Hiring a professional really is the best option when making a move. Because professionals have better equipment, are trained how to lift and move things, and are insured.

Your family may have good intentions but may not themselves be physically capable of doing all the work. Of course, if you have a large extended family which includes numerous husky teens, then asking family can make sense, assuming they can make it.

But they may not live close enough or would rather pay for the moving to be done by professionals. There are folks like Bud who want to "save money instead of paying someone" but this is one of those times when it's not a good idea. Items (or *people*) can be damaged.

Some seniors may hesitate letting their family help them pack or move because they fear that the family might "sneak something out" and toss it. This needs to be addressed early in the process of re-sizing (see Chapter 1). If you haven't done so already, now is the time to sit down and sort!

Family vs Professionals: Pricing

The time when family input becomes most influential is usually when discussing a list price. If you believe you need or want all family members to agree, please consider getting an appraisal. Because there usually is one person, maybe two, who will cling to their opinions and refuse to agree with the rest.

An appraisal is done by a licensed appraiser and is considered the gold standard for valuing a home. It will trump a real estate agent's Market Analysis, even though we try to use the same methods as appraisers. I want to stress, *agents are not appraisers.* Because the appraiser is the expert, their work will also supersede all family members' opinions.

Home sellers can make the mistake of asking their children who live in other states (or even locally) for advice as to pricing, instead of relying on the professional agent or appraiser they hired. I recall one seller with a daughter in CA and one in NYC who asked their input as to a good starting price. Of course, WI prices are nowhere near the prices in those places!

It's tempting to ask those you love for advice, but when it comes to real estate, this is not a good practice even if they live locally. Because they are not real estate professionals or appraisers.

Even if they have a real estate license, if they live elsewhere, they won't know the local market. For example, I've seen Milwaukee-area agents list houses in Sheboygan at Milwaukee prices, and those houses don't sell well if at all.

To start with, family members will have an emotional tie which can color their thinking. One time, a relative of a seller suggested a price that was 35% above known appraised value! Obviously, if the house were listed at that price, it wouldn't sell.

Even supposing it got an inflated offer that matched the price, it's doubtful that the new appraisal (from the buyer's bank) would be much different than the old one. And homes *must* appraise so the buyer can get the loan.

NOTE: *I repeat, a Market Analysis is not an Appraisal.* Once you have the appraisal, you can have confidence in pricing your home close to that value.

CHAPTER FIVE
Listing The House

Getting the Home Ready

If you've had time to prepare before calling an agent, you may already have packed or removed many items from the house. Even so, there may still be more de-cluttering and/or "staging" to do. Each house is different, but generally a home should look lived in but not *too* lived in.

Staging doesn't always mean having to hire a professional stager to come in and redo the house. Not one of my listings has ever used a professional stager.

Often it can be as simple as removing knick knacks or moving a piece of furniture. An experienced agent will be able to make suggestions. Resisting these suggestions has the potential to make the house less show-worthy, so please consider them carefully.

At times there can be bigger projects to do, such as painting or repairs. Please remember that you don't have to do it all yourself! As discussed in Chapter 4, it's tempting to try if you've been fiercely independent your whole life, but now is one time you can afford to ask for help.

Otherwise, you could get bogged down like Bob or injured like Bud. Or simply end up feeling stressed and exhausted, unable to enjoy planning what you'll do in your new place.

Enlist the help of family, friends or handymen. At this point in life, you owe it to yourself not to have to do it all alone. And set a deadline for having these projects done, so that procrastination doesn't sneak in and rob you of even more time.

Can You Sell "As-is"?

When people ask me this, I always respond, "Of course, if you don't mind an as-is price." Usually, people who want to sell as-is, mean that they want full market price for a home that needs repairs. It won't happen; I know from experience.

Approximately 32% of all listings I've had were homes that had been on the market prior but didn't sell. In every case I was able to pinpoint what the problem was, and it wasn't always price!

Based on my experiences, the two most important things anybody can do to help their chances of selling are 1) make obviously needed repairs and 2) *paint*. Paint is the cheapest way to make a property appealing and can literally make the difference between selling and not selling!

Case 1: Tried 4 times to sell; had a "designer" color that no other agent told them was the problem. They thought they had to install granite countertops and replace the kitchen floor, but all they needed was paint. Sold in 5 days, because I advised them to paint

---

Case 2: Tried 1 time to sell; had a yellow-cabinet kitchen. (People dislike yellow, especially that shade of yellow). I advised to paint white; the house sold.

Case 3: Tried to sell 3 times; had wallpaper in kitchen & baths. Nobody had told them to get rid of it. Removed the paper when I advised them to, & it sold in 5 days.

Some repairs will need to be made for insurance reasons. For example, insurance companies will be hesitant to insure a place with shingles so old they look like cornflakes. What that means is the buyer's lender won't issue the loan, because the buyer can't get insurance. No loan, no sale.

If money is tight, there are ways to get the roof done and then pay later out of proceeds. Each case is different; sometimes escrowing money is involved. Just remember, I know how to help you tackle a problem like that.

When considering making repairs or touch ups, you will need to examine cost vs benefit. The project that will net the biggest return on investment is installing a new roof (100% according to NAR, NARI, and Freddie Mac).

Too-old roofs must be replaced in order to sell…unless a cash buyer is out there somewhere. Even then, they will likely offer a discounted price because they will need to install a new roof for insurance purposes.

Can't the Buyer Fix It?

I've had countless folk ask me, "Why can't the buyer just fix it the way *they* want it?" Well, the buyer can, but you need to understand there are different types of buyers. The buyers who are willing to take an "as-is" house are expecting to get what they consider a *deal*. Their rationale is, "If I'm putting in the work to paint, install new floors, fix the broken sink, and replace the rotten window, then I won't pay as much."

On the other hand, many buyers today do not have the time, inclination, or even skill level to do any of those things, and they want a place they can just come home to. They may be a couple working three or four jobs between them or have side things going on that take their time.

These buyers are in the majority, and they will pay more, but they expect more also.

Buyers are always comparing. If there are two identical homes, but one has holes in the flooring, old leaky windows, and bright lime green paint on the walls, it won't be as appealing as one with new flooring, replaced windows, and neutral colors. The lime green home can't realistically hope to get the same price as the other one.

I've seen in real-time how a holey floor or wallpaper can negatively affect the price by **more** than what it would have cost to replace them! One fact I've observed is that décor can hurt the buyer's impression more than actual structural issues, because many people can't see past what's right in front of them. I've had buyers pass up solid homes with old décor and flooring in favor of "lipstick on a pig" properties that merely *looked* nice!

What Do Buyers Like?

In general, buyers will focus on three features: flooring, kitchen, and bathroom. The very first room they see is also important.

A local agent will be able to tell you what the latest trends are and give suggestions as to how to make the home appeal to the largest number of buyers. Of course, you do not have to implement *any* of those ideas, but at least you'll have the information needed to make informed decisions.

Take care! Don't plan on over-improving the property. Always keep in mind *cost doesn't equal value*. In other words, an appraiser assigns a value to an improvement that is not the same as the cost to complete it. The exception is a new roof.

Overwhelming?

Getting a home ready to sell doesn't have to be overwhelming. There is help out there! Even if there is no family around to assist, there are volunteer groups, grants, and other resources to help you. Use the ADRC information that's there; the resources listed are amazing. Reach out to the community.

I know one homeowner that called the local Boy Scouts for help clearing out her place. Another called the local school for some structural help because the shop teacher would take his class and do projects like that. A third had to stay temporarily in a motel while waiting to move into the new place and got food from Meals on Wheels for that time.

Of course, a real estate agent is an invaluable resource, because we know people. Handyman? Plumber? Clean-out? Furniture storage? Painter? Electrician? Floor installer? Landscaper? Roofer? We know them all! Some of these tradesmen are also willing to do deals for a homeowner with a limited income, as a way of giving back to the community.

Listing the Property: Price

When you put your home on the market, you will need to base your marketing decisions on data. A good real estate agent should be able to show you both past sales ("comps") and your current competition. When searching comps, it's been somewhat traditional to use just three to four. But I believe the best practice is to use *all* data points, as many as turn up, because the more data points, the more statistically significant the data becomes.

I always show people what past sales were and provide information on the current competition. These should be separate data sets in my opinion, because nobody knows how much the competition will actually sell for. (I believe my job is not to dictate to you what to list the house at, but rather to provide data and advice).

Competition needs to be considered in developing a strategy for price. Because the last thing you want is for your house to help sell the competition!

It can be tempting to put a higher price on your property than the data indicates. Often this is an emotional response to selling a well-loved home. Please don't do it! Especially when your competition may look better to buyers and be priced lower than your own property. Remember, *buyers are always comparing.* An agent should know what buyers like and be able to tell you if your décor will pose a barrier for buyers.

NOTE: Beware any agent who simply asks what you want and then immediately tells you that "this is what you can get." Flat-fee agents often do this because they don't have the expertise to do the research involved. I know this because decades before entering the real estate world, we'd ignorantly tried one of those, and were unable to sell until we listed with a full-service agent.

> A seller listed higher than the comps indicated and got an offer at that higher price. However, the appraiser for the lender indicated that the price needed to be adjusted. The first thing I did was to see if there were any comps that justified the offer price, to ascertain *if* the appraisal could be challenged. It couldn't. In fact, using different comps than the appraiser would have resulted in an even *lower* price!

The next day, I met with the seller to explain the position. At first, she denied it. "That can't be true! Impossible!" Then she was angry. "I'm reporting him to the state!" (Referring to the appraiser). Then she kept saying "My house is special" and asking, "Why can't the buyer take out two loans?" She was going through the *stages of decision making* triggered by the issue of the low appraisal.

I told her that the sale just wouldn't happen if she didn't adjust the price. If she wanted to cancel the contract, she could, but doing that still would not sell the house. I left forms for both options (canceling vs adjusting) and said I'd be back the next day.

When she'd had time to think it over, she was able to understand that in order for the buyers to buy, they needed a loan, and that in order to get the loan, the house had to appraise. She agreed to adjust the price.

Ambitious vs Competitive: The Market Always Talks

What if you price ambitiously and you get no offers? Or even no *showings*? What if all the feedback from buyers is "too high"? The market always talks, and in this scenario, it is screaming that the price is inaccurate.

The longer a house sits on the market, the more "shopworn" it becomes, until buyers are convinced "there must be something wrong with it." Don't be like the homeowner that had 67 showings, with feedback after each one stating, "way too high." That house never did sell.

Conversely, some homeowners who bought or built decades ago, won't believe an agent that suggests a higher price than they'd imagined. One couple told me their target price, which I knew was just too low. They became very worried and anxious when I practically insisted they needed to price above a certain point.

Fortunately, they listened and we actually had a bidding war. It sold for above list price because even at that price point, their home was still priced competitively. The market was talking.

A colleague of mine was not so fortunate. He advised a couple that they could ask "X." They were aghast. "Noooo, that can't possibly be true! It won't sell for that much!" Even though he tried to show them the data, they were so convinced he was "lying just to get a listing" that they hired another agent.

Why You Can't Trust Zillow

Probably everyone has heard of Zillow and their *Zestimates*. But basing a pricing decision on the Zestimate is risky because Zillow simply is not accurate. I have discovered that in some parts of the country, e.g. AZ, there are giant subdivisions with cookie-cutter homes. These are so similar that Zillow could take average sales and come up with something that's not too far off.

Our situation in WI is radically different. There is much less uniformity. And I can prove that Zillow changes their Zestimate to match what is shown in the MLS.

For example, there was a house that Zillow said was worth $270K before it was listed. After listing, Zillow said it was worth $342K. The house actually appraised-and sold-for $300K. The *day of closing*, Zillow claimed that the value was $291K!!!

Another example is a Zestimate for $290K prior to listing. The house was listed high, at $350k, and then Zillow claimed it was worth $356K! It actually sold for $310K. Right after closing Zillow said the place was worth $316K. These examples should be enough of an illustration that Zillow merely has an algorithm that *chases* what the agents, who do the actual market analysis, enter into the MLS.

The most important fact to bear in mind, is that a bank will **never - I repeat, never - use a Zestimate,** as appraised value. Lenders know Zestimate quite literally makes things up.

Tax Assessed Value or Square Foot Formula

Many people confuse the tax assessed value with appraised value, or they develop their own "special formula" to calculate a list price. They may know what a neighbor's home recently sold for, then look up the tax records. They calculate a ratio of assessed to sold price, and then try to apply it to their own property.

This is woefully inaccurate for several reasons. First, tax assessments are for paying taxes. Period. They really have nothing to do with what price a house can be sold for, despite the "fair market value" words seen on the tax roll. The fair market value is there as a basis for the municipality to get money.

Second, applying some sort of fancy ratio doesn't take into account the differences between homes. For example, a ranch built in 1995 will be assessed differently than a farmhouse built in 1880, even if they are in the same neighborhood. I had a seller of an old home that tried a fancy calculation based on the ranch price; it came out much higher than what his (much older) home actually could sell for.

Third, square footage must be taken into account. Smaller homes will not be assessed as highly as bigger ones, although I've noticed they tend to sell for more per square foot. This is also why using a square foot formula doesn't work. Price per square foot is used when building new, but using it to try to calculate your price, based on a neighbor's sale, ignores condition, lot size, features, home size, and decor differences.

Seasons

Certain seasons tend to favor sellers; others favor buyers. MLS data indicates that sales start to rise in March every year, continue to increase until mid-summer, and then taper off after August. Sales lag behind listing dates due to the time it usually takes for buyers' loans to process, for their own homes to get sold, or for them to give notice to their landlords. Therefore, the best time to list a home is surprisingly early in the year.

There are advantages to listing in winter for those with less than stellar landscaping because nobody expects the yard to look great. Plus, any buyer out looking in fifteen below temps is truly serious, so you know they mean business if they book a showing. However, the right time to list is when it fits *your* schedule, no matter the season.

Time on Market

When listing a home, what you *don't* want is a long DOM (days on market). Some people believe they can list high "and we can always come down later" but this strategy usually backfires. This is because a longer DOM doesn't look good to buyers.

They think to themselves, "There must be something wrong with that place because it's been on the market so long." Then when the price drops, they feel justified in their suspicions. Especially in a hot seller's market, high DOM is disastrous.

Benchmarks for DOM are the first five days, the first three weeks, and the first six weeks. The reason the first five DOM are so important is because that's when a house gets the most buyer attention.

In a hot seller's market, offers should come in within the first five days. It means buyers want to snap it up before someone else does. It does *not* mean the house was priced too low, but rather reflects the urgency buyers feel when they've been waiting for *the one* and it suddenly pops up.

In a buyer's market, DOM will be understandably longer, because there is a lot of competition among sellers for the few buyers out there. But any time your DOM is longer than the market average, you will need to reconsider your pricing strategy.

When there is an extended DOM, the likelihood increases that the house will eventually sell for less than what it could have got if priced competitively at the beginning. I've seen it happen too many times. Every agent that's been in the business long enough has seen this phenomenon, yet some sellers just don't believe that it happens this way. Trust us, it does!

CHAPTER SIX
Selling The House

Getting Showings

You did your homework. The house is on the market. Now begins a potentially stressful time. If you are still living in the home, you will need to keep it in "show-worthy" condition, which some people may find difficult. There are ways around this: you do not have to stay there in order for showings to happen.

One method is to move into the new place first. This works well when there is enough money to pay for the new place while still having the old one. Another option is to camp out with relatives or go on a vacation.

If you want or need to stay there, you can request how many hours' notice you will need. The agent will then ensure the showing app won't let people book showings too soon. Don't worry about the technical aspects of the showing app. If it truly doesn't work, all requests can go to the agent who will then call you.

Getting Offers

If your house is priced competitively, you can expect multiple offers in a seller's market. This is because "everyone wants to buy the house that someone else is after too." Depending on how hot the market is, there could be two or eight...or even more.

Getting offers right away, or over asking, does not mean you priced too low! On the contrary, getting an offer fast indicates that your price was competitive enough to attract a buyer that was ready to go. There is a saying, rooted in reality, that "Homes that sell fast, sell for top dollar." Offers written in a seller's market will strongly favor the sellers, because multiple buyers are crawling over each other to get the house.

At times sellers become ambitious when it's a seller's market and decide to list at the top of the range of potential price points. It's never wise to do this in a neutral or buyer's market, but sellers can get away with it if the market is hot. What I've seen is that these listings do take longer to get offers, but still may sell for full price. Usually there is only one offer.

In a buyer's market, the seller may have to wait quite a while to get an offer because there are so many houses for buyers to choose from. Offers in a buyer's market will have terms that strongly favor the buyers, because if they don't get what they want, they'll just choose another property.

Should you take the first offer that comes along? Statistically speaking, yes. This is because there is a *buying cycle*. What this means is that buyers will typically view between eight to twelve houses before deciding to make an offer. (Keeping the buying cycle in mind, that also means there will be eight to twelve showings before getting an offer).

Therefore, if a buyer is making an offer, they've already been through the cycle and are serious about buying. (In a buyer's market, there may be many more homes viewed by buyers because they have so many homes to choose from). So the first offer is often the best one; this is a well-known truism.

The first offer should not necessarily be ignored even if it's not what you were hoping for. Because that buyer is serious! When there are multiple offers, the best one might be the third of six that come in on the same day, so the truism that the first is best is not to be taken literally.

Chuck declined the first offer he got, because he wanted more money. As time went on, more people viewed the home, and he received five more offers, each successively lower, until the final offer was $45K less than the first. He ended up taking the house off the market.

Of course, there are times when the first offer is not the best. This is most likely to happen when the house has already been sitting on the market for a while and may also have had a price adjustment. A buyer who's been watching knows that the price dropped and wants to see how low they can go. In this case, often the seller will try a counter-offer. It's best to avoid having to face this by pricing competitively at the beginning.

Responding to Offers

You will respond to offers based on how many you get. In a bidding war situation, you will have more than one to choose from. In this scenario, you will likely pick the best one and reject the others. What constitutes "best" isn't always the price. Variables include terms of the offer, who the lender is, and what loan type the buyer is using.

Often a home will get just one offer. Remember, one is all it takes to sell a home! If the offer has terms that you don't like, you can send a counter-offer to the buyer, who then can accept, counter, or reject the counter you made. This can go on like a game of ping pong until either one party accepts a counter or decides to let the deal drop and walk away. Until a counter-offer is accepted, there is no deal, so counters should be used with discretion.

Sometimes there could be multiple offers, with none standing out as especially good. In this case, a seller may decide to use a *multiple counter proposal* that gets sent to all the buyers at once. Then they have to respond to the proposal, and the seller gets the final say. This is potentially risky because if *all* the buyers decide not to accept the multiple counter, the seller ends up with no offers at all.

Accepted Offer

Once an offer is accepted, the buyers' work starts in earnest. They have to schedule an inspection (if included in the offer), apply for their loan, deliver earnest money, pay the lender for their appraisal, schedule a mover, call utilities, and start packing.

Sellers also have to pack and call utilities for final readings. This is why it's best to start downsizing or packing before even listing a home: there will be less to do later on. There are senior moving companies that specialize in working for the senior population.

Sometimes people procrastinate downsizing or packing, and then get in a panic because they have to have all their things out of the house by the closing date. Some have even rented storage units. This may be a temporary solution but remember, it costs money every month. If you do end up using one, set a deadline for yourself to sort through the stored items. You might be surprised to find you really *don't* need all those things.

Closing (i.e. Sale)

Once the day of closing arrives, be prepared for strong emotions. You might experience relief, sadness, anticipation, or a feeling of unreality. You may even find yourself briefly going through the *stages of decision making* again. But this is not a time to look back; it's a time to focus on the future!

After closing, it's wise to resist the temptation to drive by the old place to see what the new owners are doing. One couple who moved from a two-story to a ranch did just that and were disappointed to see that the yard wasn't as well-maintained as when they'd owned it. But they were philosophical about it, unlike another seller who drove by her old home as often as she could. This kept her from enjoying her new surroundings at first.

Whatever your new situation, it's time to make the most of it. Remember, each new day is the first day of the rest of your life. It's meant to be enjoyed.

About the Author

A native of West Allis, WI, Emily met & married "A" in the UK. They came to the US with four children and settled in WI. She earned a BSN from UW-Milwaukee, and obtained her nursing license in 1996, shortly before her fifth child was born. She currently lives outside Kiel Wisconsin.

Her nursing background encompasses nursing home, MedSurg, surgery center, home health, and ER, in which specialty she spent 22 years. She also served as a trainer for staff at a local CBRF and worked per diem in nursing homes during her tenure in ER.

Emily has done extensive study in Real Estate beyond the requirements needed to obtain a real estate license. Areas of focus include the Military Relocation Professional and Senior Real Estate Specialist, as well as many other designations.

In late 2023, Emily became a Homes for Heroes Agent Affiliate. Homes for Heroes is a program that was developed after 9/11 by a group in MN. H4H agents donate part of their compensation to the organization, which then provides a "Hero Reward" to recipients after closing. The Hero populations include people who work or worked in Education, EMS/Fire, Healthcare, Law enforcement, and Military. And even support staff qualify! To find out more about Homes for Heroes and how it works, go to www.ishomesforheroesascam.com

Contact Information

www.linkedin.com/in/emilymatthewsrealtor

(Emily Matthews RE Agent)

www.facebook.com/EmilyMatthewsWIRealtor

(Emily Matthews RE Agent)

www.youtube.com/@EmilyMatthewsRealtor

(Emily Matthews RE Agent)

www.emilymatthewsreagent.com

Phone Number: (920) 286-0570